Rockin' Life From Home

Success Strategies To Balance Family Life
And Working From Home

Cindy C. Baker

Copyright © 2020 Cindy Baker.

All rights reserved. This book or any portion thereof may not be reproduced or used in any manner whatsoever without the express written permission of the publisher, except for the use of brief quotations in a book review.

Web addresses and links may have changed since publication and my no longer be valid.

This is a work of non-fiction. Names and characters are fictitious and are of the creation of the author's imagination. Any resemblance to people, living or dead, or actual events are purely coincidental.

The information, including but not limited to text, graphics, images, and other material contained in the book, is for informational purposes only. The intent of the author is to offer general information for self-help and well-being. It is not intended to be a substitute for professional medical advice, diagnosis, or treatment. Always seek the advice of your physician or other qualified health care provider with any questions you may have regarding a medical and/or psychological condition or treatment.

ISBN: 978-1-7358457-0-8

1st edition, September 2020

Contents

PREFACE 1
INTRODUCTION The Characters in the Story 4
CHAPTER 1 Group Session #1 Journaling as a tool in self-discovery 12
    Week One Information packet 25
    Keeping a Journal 26
    Journal Entry: 27
    Observation: 28
    Managing What You Cannot Control 29
    Gratitude Journaling 30
CHAPTER 2 Group Session #2 Mindfulness in Action 32
    5 Minute Mindfulness Activity 45
    Week 2 Information Packet 46
    Replacing Negative Thoughts 48
    Mindfulness Tips 49
CHAPTER 3 Session #3 Communication & Time Management 50
    Week 3 Information Packet 65
    Effective Communication for the Whole Family 66
    Time Management Success 68
CHAPTER 4 Final Group Session #4 Boundary Setting and Beyond 70
    Week 4 Information Packet 88
    Maintaining Balance 90
    Goal Setting 93
    The program is over, now what? 95
Epilogue 96
About the Author 98

Cindy C. Baker

PREFACE

Have you ever felt the familiarity of home and yet your routine at home has been totally turned upside down? The unexpected has happened and you find yourself living and working from home in a way you would not have imagined. You must re-invent your day to accommodate your new schedule. You must find new ways of coping with this change in your life.

Life can feel like a roller coaster with ups and downs, twists and bends and turns that even flip you upside down. You find yourself inviting the excitement that helps you feel alive and vibrant. However, the roller coaster can be equally as terrifying. How well you endure depends on your ability to adapt to change.

Change can be quite challenging. However, you can learn strategies for success that will catapult you from struggling to thriving in your new work from home life.

I invite you into a world of five characters that have been thrown into a new lifestyle of living and working from home. They each have their own set of challenges to overcome in their new roles. They are facing new demands on their time as they seek to balance work and family. Each have decided to join a stress management group designed for adults who are new to the work from home environment. They will meet with a Certified Life Design Coach weekly for a month to focus on how to manage and adapt to this new change. The coach will help them along the way learn to set good boundaries, communicate their needs better, establish new routines and, of course, reduce stress. They will learn valuable mindfulness techniques that will help them to better cope. Follow along to see the characters transform their lives for the better. Discover what works and does not work for them. See how this group from different walks of life find common ground and form a kinship that lasts far beyond the group.

Adjusting to new and unexpected changes takes time. I have counseled and coached people on how to successfully navigate change for over twenty years. I have helped hundreds of people struggling to find their inner peace and joy. Even though the characters are completely fictitious (even the coach) the guidance and tools provided are not. We learn best through storytelling so I have written this book as a story embedding self-help strategies in which you can immediately benefit. These are the same strategies I have taught throughout my career that benefit clients the most. Consider this a self-help book told in story format. As you read this book, I strongly encourage you to have an open mind and try the recommended strategies along with the characters. Imagine being a part of the group and participating in each activity. Have a journal handy to write down your experiences. As with anything in life the more effort you put into something the more benefit you will receive. If you want to feel better and thrive then read ahead and discover how you too can experience greater peace, balance, and happiness in your life.

Rockin' Life From Home

INTRODUCTION
The Characters in the Story

Ginger, The Coach

Bustling with enthusiasm Ginger walks into the office and shouts, "Happy Monday!" to her receptionist, who barely looks up over the mounting paperwork to grunt a "Good Morning" in return. Accustomed to Suzie's response, Ginger gives her a warm smile, stifles a giggle, and heads down the corridor towards her office.

As you open the door into Ginger's office you see walls bathed in warm colors of muted brown and orange that catch your attention and invite you into the space like a cozy blanket. Two large windows provide just the right amount of sunshine in to keep the tall palm plants flourishing. On one side of the room a long light blue overstuffed couch with matching loveseat form an "L" shape. Two cream pinstriped chairs opposite them mirror a casual living room you may find at a friend's home. The other side of the room, the only part of the room that looks like an office, has a beautiful wood secretary desk with ornate carvings and claw feet. Rich landscape paintings add the finishing touch to the space. New clients often comment on the space and how welcoming it feels. This is exactly what Ginger hoped for when she first designed the space years ago.

Ginger looked over the office making sure it was prepped and ready for the day. Briefly stopping at the couches to fluff the pillows, she silently gave thanks to the day and appreciation of her full client schedule.

Jerry

Meet Jerry, a 47-year-old executive that has spent more hours at work than at home. He has a lot of responsibility running the sales division of a midsize communications company. Jerry has worked his way up the corporate ladder putting in massive number of hours. Jerry enjoys his work and gets great satisfaction when his team lands new accounts. Amongst his team he is known as a hard worker with high expectations. He puts in the hours and expects the same from his employees. He runs a tight but fair ship and enjoys his play time. When his team meets their monthly quota, he takes them to the golf course to celebrate.

Mary, his wife of 20 years, is a kind and generous soul who is understanding of Jerry's work schedule. After watching his single mother struggle working two jobs to provide for him and his brother, he vowed to himself that he would work hard to provide for this family. Jerry met Mary in college. While Jerry was a business management major, Mary was studying to be a teacher. They met on campus at one of Jerry's fraternity parties. They have been together ever since.

They got married a few years after college. Once Mary became pregnant with their first child, she retired from teaching to be a stay at home mother. Their boy is now a senior in high school, and they have a daughter, age fourteen.

Mary is happy and content being the primary caretaker in the family. Mary's nurturing tendencies balances out

Jerry's occasional grouchiness. She is the yin to Jerry's yang. Jerry and Mary have a deep appreciation and love for each other that has deepened over the years.

Jerry was not prepared for what he was about to endure. His "roller coaster" turned upside down when Mary's mother, who lives alone in Montana, fell, and broke her hip. Mary felt conflicted over going to help her mom and leaving her husband to take care of their kids. Jerry encouraged Mary to go because it was the right thing to do even though he was feeling a bit queasy on the inside. His hour-long commute to work would put him too far from home right now. He needed to be more accessible for the kids. Jerry must now work from home while his wife is out of town. How is Jerry going to manage the kids, take care of the home and work?

Ann

Ann is a 35-year-old with high energy and spunky nature. She makes a good living as a corporate trainer for a midsize construction company which has several office branches throughout the country. Ann routinely travels to the various branches as needed. Ann loves her job as she feeds off the energy in the office along with the demanding work schedule.

Ann's husband, Todd, is a loving, supportive husband, and father to their two children. Fortunately, Todd is an accountant for a small company that affords him typical 8 to 5 work hours.

Last Monday, Ann walked into the office for business as usual. Much to her surprise she was informed that her local branch office was closing. The company decided to downsize to cut back on their expenses. The local employees had a choice of relocating to one of their other branches or working from home. Ann wasn't about to move since her and her husband's families lived locally. So, she had no other option but to move her office into her home. Ann was not happy about this at all. She loved her family, but she also loved interacting with everyone at the office, as she considered them her second family. She would be home alone most of the day while her children were in school. How is extroverted, high-energy Ann going to adapt?

Stephanie

With a toddler in tow, Stephanie, 28, is struggling with managing motherhood and running her home-based business. Her husband, Jessie, is concerned for her. He sees her stressing herself out trying to tackle too many things in a day. He knows they could really use the money that Stephanie is earning but recognizes it is tough on her to both take care of their newborn and operate a new business.

Stephanie realizes she is stressed but hides it the best she can. She starts her day early with long "to do" lists. She likes everything in her home to be neat and tidy. Stephanie likes to have all the housework done before Jessie arrives home from work. That way she can have quality family time.

Stephanie adores their baby girl and has easily taken to motherhood. Stephanie babysat a lot when she was a teenager and is a natural at caring for kids. She feels overwhelmed trying to meet her own expectations. How can she keep this pace up?

Miles

A few years ago, Miles created a study prep app that ended up being successful enough that it covered his living expenses while in college. If anyone had a tech question, they knew who to ask. Miles could often be found on campus under a gigantic oak tree immersed in his laptop.

Preferring the company of his computer over people, he feels awkward communicating with actual people. He mostly keeps to himself. In his senior year, his roommate helped him out by introducing him to Lisa. They fell in love and married shortly after graduation.

Two years later, at age 24, Miles is a father to a 6-month-old girl and is embarking on a new plan. He recently resigned from a small tech firm to launch his own online business. He converted their third bedroom into office space. He had great plans to put in long hours making his dream a reality. However, his wife is so happy to have him home that she keeps interrupting him all throughout the day! How is Miles going to balance home and work life?

Rayna

Rayna is a busy single mom juggling between working full time as an Executive Assistant and caring for her three children, ages 8, 10 and 14. Rayna is a proud, strong woman who believes in living life honestly and doing the "right" thing.

Her cell phone rang at work. It was the principal of her oldest son Elijah's school calling again regarding his disruptive behaviors and poor grades. Elijah has been receiving detention for not paying attention and cracking jokes in class. "He is a pretty funny kid but there is a time and place for humor," she told a close colleague at work.

Rayna spent her lunch time picking Elijah up from school. Something had to be done to help Elijah, but what could she do?

CHAPTER 1
Group Session #1
Journaling as a tool in self-discovery

With anticipated enthusiasm, Ginger returned from lunch for her first stress management class this afternoon. She designed the program based on some of the common challenges her previous clients have faced. She wants to help her clients in a deeper way by introducing people to each other who are also struggling with adapting to working from home. The group would have a chance to get to know each other, gain valuable education and support in a way that individual sessions alone do not offer.

Ginger took some of the best, most current stress management techniques in psychotherapy, positive psychology and coaching to use with the group. When the class completed, the members were welcome to attend a free monthly support group at the office.

She remembered when she first opened her coaching practice. She had been working for years as a counselor within a large community counseling agency but wanted to move into the coaching field. She felt a bit lost in branching out on her own and was not sure of her next steps. A friend of hers recommended she speak to a business coach she knew named Paula. She was hesitant at first but contacted her and briefly discussed her dilemma. She was unsure of what direction to take her practice. She was worried about getting enough clients to pay the bills. Even though she was super excited about this new chapter in her life she recognized she felt overwhelmed and stressed. Coach Paula ended up being a helpful, wise mentor who helped her grow her practice.

She recalled Paula teaching her a powerful visual exercise. Paula instructed her to close her eyes. She then asked her to visualize her perfect day of work. See yourself walking down the hall to greet your new client. What does your client look like, male or female? What age? Imagine your client sitting down in your office and chatting. What does your client say? What is important to your client? What challenges does your client have? What goals does your client want to achieve? Imagine all the little details of your session. Hear yourself speaking about topics of interest. Consider your level of expertise. What do you enjoy teaching your client? What type of personality does your client have? Run the entire session from beginning to end in your mind. Notice how you feel when the session is over.

When Ginger opened her eyes, she felt renewed enthusiasm about her decision of opening her private practice. She had greater clarity and knew what she wanted to do. Instead of feeling stressed, she felt energized. She knew she wanted to focus on helping clients reduce their stress. She had already helped others at the counseling center where she used to work and now she could bring those same skills into her private coaching practice.

Ginger is forever grateful to the insight she gleamed from her coaching sessions. Every so often, she still reaches out to Paula when she wants a supportive ear in helping her make new changes in her practice.

With her goals in sight, Ginger carefully set up her practice to attract the people she most enjoyed working with. She built her business plan based on how she visualized her practice. Every decision she made from marketing to networking was influenced with her ideal client in mind.

Now, years later Ginger acknowledged the beauty of her plan. She had indeed designed and built her business just like she had envisioned years ago. Her passion comes through her work and her clients feel that she genuinely wants to help them reduce stress and create a life they love.

Snapping out of her reminiscing, Ginger placed a welcome platter of snacks and bottles of water out for her group. She had carefully screened them in advance and felt this was going to be a vibrant group of people.

They all arrived on time and helped themselves to the snack tray and settled into the space. Even though Ginger had met each one they did not know each other. The room was awkwardly quiet but Ginger was confident that it would not stay this way. She had run many kinds of groups in the past and was familiar with group dynamics.

"Welcome to the group everyone. I want to thank each of you for carving time out of your busy day to come here. I also encourage you to give a warm thanks to yourself for taking this opportunity to focus on your wellness and personal growth," said Ginger. She passed out "Week One Informational Packets to each member (informational packets are at the end of each chapter). After briefly going over the ground rules and expectations, it was time for the members to share a bit about themselves and what made them choose this group.

Ann spoke first. "I am so happy I found this group. I am used to being around people all day, however, now I am at home and it is driving me crazy! I guess I should back up a bit and tell you a little about myself. I love, love, love being a corporate trainer. It is the best job! I was fortunate enough to land this position right out of college. Several days of month I travel to our various satellite offices. It keeps things fresh, ya know? I have a wonderful husband, Todd, who is an accountant and two beautiful children, Bobby, age 10 and Dee Dee, age 8. A few weeks ago, my boss makes this announcement that they are shutting down our office to reduce some of their overhead costs. They gave the staff the option to relocate to another active office or work from home. Well, the closest office is a four-hour drive from home. It was not the best option for me, so I chose to work from home. I never envisioned working at home. I am way too much of a people person to be at home all day. My husband goes to his job and the kids go to school and I am left home all by myself. So, when I found this group, I thought it might be useful in helping me adjust to my new work life." Ginger thanked Ann for her openness and invited others to share their stories as well.

With the ice broken by Ann, Rayna chimed in and admitted she was hesitant to sign up for this program. "I was raised to be a strong woman and to take care of my family business on my own. Growing up we did not talk about our troubles outside of the home. We simply did what needed to be done. It was hard for me to admit I needed some help in managing what is going on at home. I am still not sure whether it is good idea that I am here. However, I am true to my word. I knew if I signed up, I would see it through to the end." Ginger acknowledged how difficult this decision to join the group must have been for Rayna. Ginger asked Rayna if she would like to share a little about what was going on at home. Rayna took a deep breath and began. "I am a single parent with three children fourteen and under. I work full-time as an executive assistant. I have an 8-year-old son, Benjamin, and a 10-year-old daughter, Mia. They are okay. They both do well in school, make good grades and all. My oldest, Elijah, who is 14 years old is another story." Rayna explained how Elijah came to be homeschooled for the remainder of the school year. "It is a lot to juggle right now," Rayna sighed.

Jerry looked around the group and decided it was his turn. "I must admit I am totally out of my element here. I am used to running a company and having staff come to me for advice, not the other way around. However, I can respect that this group may be able to provide knowledge that could help in dealing with my situation." Jerry told the group about his wife, Mary, having to abruptly leave to take care of her mother in Montana while leaving Jerry to care for their two kids. "Mary left me a lot of instructions," Jerry chuckled. "She also insisted I attend this group. After being together for 20 years, she knows me well. She knew I would not reach out for help even though I needed it. She was right too. I rely on her so much when it comes to taking care of our family. She excels at it. It is because of her that I have been so successful in my career. I can leave every day for work and know Mary will take care of the home and our kids. With today's technological advances I can work pretty much anywhere. However, I still prefer to be in the office. I have to approach my team differently since I am not physically present. My biggest challenge is fulfilling both mine and Mary's roles while she is away."

"I guess I will go next," Stephanie volunteered. Stephanie cleared her throat and began. "My husband, Jessie, encouraged me to attend this group. He is worried about me. He noticed I am more stressed than usual. Basically, I am struggling with getting everything done each day. I have a six-month-old baby girl, Bethany, at home right now whom I absolutely adore. My best friend agreed to watch her so I could be here today. I also work from home. It is hard managing my work and taking care of Bethany which, both seem to need my full-time attention at the same time! It is a lot of responsibility." Stephanie shrugged her shoulders to signal she was done and looked at the only member left to talk.

Miles squirmed in his chair as he contemplated what to say. "I started working from home about two months ago," Miles explained. "My wife, Lisa, takes care of our daughter, Zoe. I am trying to get my online business up and running but being at home has been distracting. Lisa keeps coming into my office and talking. She talks about what needs to be done around the house, she asks me what I want for dinner or she shares what Zoe is doing. It is a lot for me to handle. I do not want to hurt her feelings, but I also need my space to work so I can support our family. I am just stressed out." The group nodded their heads in understanding. Miles did not realize how tense he had been bottling up his emotions for so long. He felt relief after voicing his thoughts.

Ginger thanked the group for sharing. She reached under her chair and pulled a wicker box and retrieved the journals she bought for them. She said, "I have found using a journal to record experiences is helpful. There is something powerful in writing down our thoughts and feelings and then re-reading them later. I strongly encourage you to actively use these to capture your progress as we move through the program. You will also use them to complete homework assignments in between sessions. There is no right or wrong way to use a journal. You can use traditional writing, bullet points, draw or doodle in your journals. Now is a good excuse to use crayons, colored pencils and pens, markers, or stickers. This is a time to tap into your own creative space. When we get bogged down with problems, we tend to rely on our logic to pull us through. But most of the time we end up dwelling on the problem versus focusing on the solution. Often it is the creative side of our brains that come up with the solutions. Journal use will reflect your deepest creative thoughts, intentions, and desires. Express yourself in your own unique way and have fun with it."

After a short break to stretch their legs, the group returned for the second half of the session. Ginger began, "Change doesn't feel comfortable for anyone. With change there is a lot of new things to get used to which can bring about stress. Most of your day is run on automatic pilot. Your brain functions to a large extent on habituated patterns. You have over sixty thousand thoughts a day and about 95% of those thoughts are the same thoughts you had yesterday. You get up every day and generally do the same routines. You do not have to relearn how to brush your teeth or drive your car each day. Thank goodness because that would be exhausting! You have built habits to make your life easier. These habits are stored in your unconscious mind. Since they work automatically, it does not take much brain power to run your daily habits. However, when you first learned your ABCs you had to go over them again and again to memorize them. You put forth effort at first until they became memorized and effortless to recall. This is the reason why change is challenging. Change brings about newness that you cannot run on automatic pilot simply because you haven't developed that habit! So, everything takes more effort and brain energy to work through. Does this make sense?"

Members nodded in agreement. Stephanie said, "That explains a lot. No wonder starting my new business and becoming a mother at the same time has been so exhausting."

Jerry added, "I think I have forgotten what learning a new skill feels like. I should take it a little easier on new employees."

With a frown Ann said, "So, it just takes some time for my life to normalize? What if I don't want it to? I mean, I don't want to work from home."

Ginger explained, "I understand. You make an excellent point Ann. It does take time to adjust to a new situation. Repeating new patterns and systems, like working from home, over time will create new habits which in turn makes your day run easier. However, there is more to it than just letting time pass. I would like you to do an exercise. Grab your journal and write down or doodle the main feeling associated with what is going on in your life right now."

Stephanie quickly reached for the colored markers in the box on the coffee table and began drawing in her journal. Ann and Rayna reached in next and began writing their words. Miles grabbed a pen and tapped his foot as he wrote. Jerry pulled out his own pen and followed suit.

A few minutes later, Ginger asked the group to share. Members listened attentively as each took their turn.

Ann wrote the word "isolated" in capital letters in her journal. She went from working in a busy office with plenty of people around her to being home alone. Stephanie doodled a stick figure of a girl with flaming red hair sticking straight up indicating feeling frantic. Rayna wrote "worried" in small black letters. In block style writing, Miles wrote "overwhelmed" and Jerry printed "lonely" on his paper. The group anxiously looked at Ginger waiting for a response. They felt vulnerable, having expressed their most raw feelings to absolute strangers. Ginger acknowledged their courage to share what was bothering them the most.

Ginger said, "What would happen if you decided to drive across the country without a road map or GPS? You would probably get lost. Without a clear plan you are directionless. If you are unaware of where you are going, then you do not know the steps that will take you to your destination. Just like driving through new territory, it is important to acknowledge where you are currently at in your life right now. Acknowledging what you are currently feeling and experiencing gives you a solid place in which to start carving out and designing what you really want. Having both the beginning and end point in mind, you can create a course of action to bring your desire into reality. Understanding your feelings, you can start practicing excellent self-care which is especially important when you face challenges. Asking yourself what you can do to feel better is essential to providing the emotional support needed to work through problems. In other words, what can you do to take care of what you most need? Jerry, let's start with you. What can help you feel less lonely?"

Jerry responded, "well, I know my wife has been pretty busy caring for her mom. I have wanted to call her several times but haven't. I didn't want to bother her. I didn't want her to worry about me either."

"I wonder if she could be feeling the same way, Jerry," mentioned Ginger.

"I don't know, but it is possible," said Jerry.

Ginger said, "there is another way of looking at it too. By not reaching out to your wife, you are denying her the opportunity to connect with you."

Jerry crinkled his brow in thought. "I hadn't thought of it like that. I suppose I could call her more often to briefly check in with her, just to say hello. Hearing her voice always makes me feel better. It would definitely help me feel less alone."

Ginger said, "I think that is a great idea, Jerry. Thank you for being a good sport and going first. Jerry was able to come up with a step he can act on right away to help him feel less lonely. I would like the rest of the group to do the same. Be sure to write them in your journals."

After a few minutes of silence, Ann shared that she could relate to Jerry's dilemma. She felt lonely and cut off from her team at work. Ann decided to use video team meetings instead of phone conferences so everyone could see each other. She also decided to take her neighbor up on her offer and start walking in the mornings with her before work.

Rayna said she would look into an online tutoring option for her son. She wanted to make sure he had the academic support he needed. Plus, it would free up some of her time during the day to focus on her job.

"Ugh, my husband was right! I do take on too much. I am sure not going to tell him that!" Stephanie said with a smile. "I don't know how to approach my day any other way though. I am so used to going at mach speed. It was hard for me to choose only one thing. I first made a list of ten steps! I know we are supposed to have one, but I got stumped. Help!" Stephanie exasperatingly slumped in her chair.

Rayna looked over at Ginger and asked, "can I say something?"

"Of course," Ginger said. "We can all learn from and support each other. That is the beauty of groups."

"Stephanie, as a single mother who always has a multitude of things I am juggling, what I have found helpful is prioritizing my tasks. Look at your list. Compare the first one to the second. Which one is more important? Now take you answer and compare it to your third item. Take that answer and compare it to the fourth item and so on. When you are finished comparing them you will have your top main task you can complete."

The group watched as Stephanie prioritized her tasks. "I did it!" Stephanie excitedly shouted. "Who knew such a simple exercise could be so helpful? This alone will help me feel less frantic. I am going to start using this every day to organize my 'to do' list. My one thing I will do this week is make Mondays my grocery shopping day. I usually go whenever I feel like it or when we are out of something. Having a set day will give me some structure."

"Sounds like a great start," Ginger said.

The group turned their heads to face Miles. Realizing he was the last to speak, Miles said, "I think I have to realize my office life at home is going to be different than what I was used to at the tech company. I must get used to more interruptions. I initially thought I would be able to get a lot more done at home and be able to meet my deadlines more quickly. Basically, I need to adjust my expectations. I am going to revisit my deadlines and push them back so I don't feel so overwhelmed."

"I think that is a good idea," Rayna encouraged, already showing signs of mothering the group.

Ginger went over the information packet and answered any questions about their assignments they were responsible for completing before the next session. Ginger encouraged members if they get stuck, they can ask a trusted family member or friend for some ideas. She reminded them small steps can make a big impact.

With each member understanding the game plan for the week, Ginger closed the session.

Cindy C. Baker

Week One Information packet

Journaling as a Tool in Self-Discovery

Welcome to the stress management course! You will receive an information packet for each of the four classes. The packet is supplemental and is designed to support what we will be talking about in each class.

Change can be scary. You are walking a path that is unknown, unchartered territory. It ignites a primal fear of uncertainty as you face a new challenge. You feel dis-ease from the lack of structure or plan. Know that this is a normal response and that it will not last long. It takes time for new routines and expectations to be established. Self-care is especially important when managing change.

(If you feel stuck and would like a support partner, consider scheduling a strategic life coaching appointment with me to help gain clarity, direction and design a course of action).

Keeping a Journal

Set aside a few minutes a day to spend with your journal. Use your journal as a platform of self-expression. Acknowledging your thoughts and feelings is the first step in supporting yourself through this change. Next follows learning and applying new skills to make this transition as smooth and as easy as possible.

As you go through this program you will gain valuable, personal insights. Be sure to include these insights in your journal as well.

Identifying Feelings

Each day note how you are feeling. Instead of being consumed by your feelings, ask yourself what you can do to help you through it so that you can shift from feeling overwhelmed to feeling empowered. Asking yourself key questions that prompt you to act will help move away from being stuck to creating opportunities for positive change.

Prioritize your to do list

Keep your task list between 5 and 10 items daily. Shoot for five if they are labor intensive and ten if they will not take too long. Rate each one in order of importance to help you decide which one to do first.

Simplify your days by scheduling your regular weekly tasks such as grocery shopping, laundry, and cleaning.

Journal Entry:

When you encounter an unexpected life change, you typically spend a lot of time ruminating on the problem. You can easily become "stuck" in the problem instead of seeking effective solutions. The goal with any challenge is to acknowledge it, take what we need from it and move through it. Easier said than done, I know! This next activity will really help you feel more empowered. Take your time with it and add to it as new thoughts come to you.

On the next page in your journal draw a line down the middle of the page. On the left side at the top write, "Things I can control" and on the right side at the top write, "Things that I cannot control." Start with simple things like the ability to choose your clothes for the day or the ability to choose what you make for dinner and build from there. Continue to fill in both sides of the list. Feel free to use as many journal pages as you like. (Note: You can download a worksheet at (www.rockinlifefromhome.com)

Observation:

What did you notice about this activity?

Which side do you spend most of your time thinking about? If you answered, the right, then it is time to retrain your brain to think in a new way. If you focus on what you cannot control, then you will feel powerless. However, if you focus more on the left side of the list, you will feel stronger and more empowered. Spend a few minutes giving thanks to your empowered list, for all the privileges that can easily be taken for granted. Make a commitment to yourself to spend more time focusing on the things that you can control, and you will find that your happiness level rises!

Cindy C. Baker

Managing What You Cannot Control

Having trouble letting go of the side you cannot control? Try this activity.

Even though I cannot control _____ (fill in from right side) I am grateful I have the ability to_____(fill in with something on the left side of the list).

Examples:

Even though I am struggling with working from home, I am grateful that I have a job.

Even though I am stressed out trying to balance work and family, I am grateful I have a loving supportive family.

Whenever you catch your mind dwelling on something out of your control, use the above technique. You may have to do this frequently at first but, in time, the thoughts most likely will subside.

Gratitude Journaling

Practicing gratitude during a challenging time will help you quickly reduce stress. Gratitude is as much a feeling as it is a thinking activity. Make sure you really feel the feelings stemming from true gratitude. Again, start simple and jot them down in your journal.

Examples:

I am grateful for this great cup of hot tea.

I am grateful for my beloved pet who is always here for me, giving me unconditional love and warming my cold feet!

I am grateful that I have clean clothes that fit in my closet.

I am grateful that my children are well.

I am grateful I have a job right now.

Typically, as you practice gratitude you will move from simple to more meaningful concepts. Begin your gratitude practice by journaling twice a day. Write 3 things you are grateful for in the morning and 3 things you are grateful for from your day. Be thankful for all things great and small, without judgment. This will help you shift from stress-based thinking to one of genuine appreciation.

Cindy C. Baker

Gratitude Journaling

Use your journal to capture what you are genuinely grateful for in your life. Practicing daily appreciation also increases life satisfaction and overall happiness. Jot down what you are grateful for in the morning upon awakening and at bedtime. Reviewing your grateful list in your head is also a great way to fall asleep!

CHAPTER 2
Group Session #2
Mindfulness in Action

The group filed in one by one and settled into their seats. Feeling more comfortable at the second meeting, the members more warmly smiled at each other and began small talk.

"Good morning everyone, "said Ginger as she passed out the informational packet for the second week." She continued to address the group. "I want to start today's discussion with a brief follow-up from last week's homework assignment. Who would like to begin?" Ann looked around at the members and then leaned forward to speak first.

"All week I was looking forward to our next session," said Ann. "Not only did I set up weekly video conferences with my staff, but I also had an informal meeting inquiring into how they were adjusting to the office closing. Some of my staff are working from home, like me, while others relocated to other satellite offices. I found out they are feeling pretty similar to me and that made me feel so much better. I also shared with them some of the things we talked about last week! Oh, and I started walking with my neighbor in the morning and it felt so good to have some fellowship with someone before work. Overall, I had a much better week. I still feel a bit isolated during the day, but it was less which was a good thing."

"Well done Ann," encouraged Ginger.

"I hope you don't mind me asking but who takes care of your kids in the morning?" Rayna inquired.

Ann knows how lucky she is to have such a supportive husband. He is a great father and wonderful husband. "Actually, my husband, Todd, gets the kids up and drives them to school every day. He has always taken care of the busy morning routine since I left the house super early each day. He is my rock! Since I am home now the kids don't have to attend the after-school program anymore. They get to ride the bus home. They are thrilled!" Ann paused and considered how hard it would be if she had to care for the kids all by herself. Facing Rayna, Ann said, "I can't imagine how I would handle being a single parent. I really admire your strength raising your children on your own."

"Thank you. I have been doing it on my own for so long I forget what it is like to have a partner," Rayna sighed. "I guess I will go next. I did some research on tutors for Elijah and I found three I am interested in interviewing. I set up appointments later this week. From our first session I realized I was also worried about how to manage the logistics of working and schooling from home. My kids share a computer upstairs in the loft. I took over the dining room as my office which is, of course, downstairs. I kept thinking, how I am I going to run up and down the stairs all day long answering questions and checking on him? When I am downstairs in the office, I would be wondering what he is doing up there. He tends to become easily distracted. Such divided attention would really hurt my productivity. And my poor knees! So, I had the kids help me set up their computer in the dining room with mine. Elijah pitched a mighty fit over it. He has this notion that home school equates to him doing whatever he wants," Rayna chuckled. "Boy, did he get a wake-up call! I was not his favorite person last weekend!" Rayna said. The members laughed along with Rayna as they could relate to the challenges of parenting.

Jerry commented, "parenting is hard work for everyone. I think that, even though Elijah doesn't like the idea, it will ultimately teach him discipline and accountability, which will serve him well in the future when he enters the workforce."

"I think it will too. Thanks Jerry," Rayna said in return.

Stephanie chimed in for the first time this morning. "Ya'll are going to laugh at me but I really tried to prioritize my list!" Stephanie dove into her humongous paisley purse and pulled out a crumpled legal-size piece of paper to show the group her numbered list. There must have been at least forty items on her to do list!

Rayna gasped, "my goodness, Stephanie; is that just for today?" Stephanie sheepishly nodded in affirmation.

"I would go crazy trying to tackle a mile-long list like that one!" Rayna said.

"That is a pretty long list even for me!" said Ann.

"My husband would agree with both of you if he were here," Stephanie anxiously said.

Ginger spoke up. "May I make a recommendation Stephanie?"

"Yes, please," replied Stephanie.

"Okay," Ginger began, "Having long to do lists can set you up for failure. Instead, setting up a realistic daily agenda ensures you will most likely get it all completed and it feels good to have a sense of achievement. Perfectionism, on the other hand is a recipe for disaster. No one is perfect and that is okay. Striving for perfection is a pursuit that is not attainable. It puts too much pressure to be something that you are not. You could say that we all are perfectly imperfect. All of us get up and do the best we can, given our circumstances and level of awareness. I recommend you do not put more than ten items a day on your list. If the items are labor intensive and require multiple steps, reduce the list to five items. What you don't finish in the day get placed on the next day to complete. Try that this week and we will check in with you at the third meeting."

Stephanie nodded and replied, "when I think about shortening my list, I actually feel better. When I considered doing it in the past, I guess I thought I was a failure...like I just couldn't handle it or something. What you are saying is that it sets me up for a greater sense of accomplishment if I do shorten my list."

Ginger asked, "and how does it feel to give yourself permission to do this?"

"Wow, it feels really good!" Stephanie said.

Ginger said, "Awesome, Stephanie! In this group, you are learning strategies that will not only reduce stress but will set you up for success as well."

Jerry leaned forward and said, "I just want to say that I can relate to Stephanie. I keep long work hours. I have gotten so used to the intensity of my schedule that I hadn't stopped to think about why I was doing it in the first place. I am at a point in my life that I don't even have to and yet I still push myself to accomplish more and more." Jerry stared at the floor in deep thought and muttered softly, "I will definitely give that some thought."

Coming out of his deep thought, Jerry took a deep breath and continued. "About my week, it was still pretty hectic. I spent most afternoons playing chauffeur for my kids, taking them to their extracurricular events. My boy, Jonathon, who's fifteen, plays baseball for his high school. He can hit that baseball like you would not believe. Out of his teammates, he has the most home runs. My daughter, Cassie, takes dance. She has been dancing as long as she has been walking! She just started high school this year. They both work hard developing their interests and they keep their grades up too. They are good kids." Jerry paused, then rubbed his hands together. "I was angry about missing an important meeting Wednesday while I was at Jonathon's baseball practice. On the way home I snapped at the kids. Cassie started crying. Jonathon didn't say a word to me the rest of the night. I know it is not their fault. I felt bad about the whole thing." Jerry shrugged his shoulders as if he was resigned to what he said next.

"After the kids were in bed, I ended up calling my wife and telling her all about it. We talked for a long time. It felt good to get some things off my chest." Jerry smiled for the first time. "The next day, I took the kids out for an early breakfast and we talked. We worked it out. Everything is okay now. Since then, my wife and I have been talking a few times a day, which has really helped."

Rayna, offering her support said, "I am glad to hear it. Juggling schedules can make you crazy sometimes."

Again, Miles was the last to participate. Feeling the pressure, Miles reported on his week. "Well," he began, "I pushed back my deadlines, but I still feel pretty stressed. My wife keeps interrupting me all throughout the day. I moved my office home to save on the rent, but I don't know if that was such a good idea after all." Miles ran his fingers through his dark hair. Patiently the group waited to hear more from Miles; however, he didn't say anything else. He simply sat there slumped in his chair.

After a considerable pause, Ginger said, "Miles, it sounds like you are having some boundary challenges at home. We are going to cover that more in the next session because it is a big part of what makes working from home a success. The work dynamics are different when you are home and learning how to successfully navigate the balance is essential to your productivity and emotional well-being." Continuing to address Miles, Ginger said, "It seems your wife means well. She just wants to connect with you. It may be helpful to carve out a small window in your workday to connect with her. When would be a good time during the day to speak with your wife, perhaps at lunch or an afternoon work break?"

Miles considered her question. "I haven't thought about it that way before. I see the hurt I cause her when I get frustrated. I would not mind lunch time and even a time in the afternoon. I don't know how to broach the subject with her. I don't want to make the situation worse. I am not so good at expressing myself. Any suggestions?" The members all turned to Ginger awaiting her response.

"I think it is important to have an honest talk with her. You could start by telling her, in order to be as productive as possible, you are trying out a new work schedule so that you can continue to provide for your family. Ask for her help in this. Tell her you function best when you have uninterrupted blocks of time to focus and concentrate. Tell her you also want to share special moments with her and your child. In order to do this, schedule lunch and an afternoon break to come out of your office every day and visit with them. Keep to your schedule and don't rely on her to tell you it is break time. Set an alarm or notification for break times if you need to."

Miles shook his head and replied, "I will give that a try."

Ginger announced breaktime and watched as the members dispersed. Miles left the room and headed outside for some fresh air. He sat down at the picnic table and pulled out his phone to check his email. Ginger hoped, in time, Miles would open up and feel more a part of the group. Rayna and Stephanie were chatting quietly by the coffee station while Jerry and Ann were chuckling as they looked out the window watching two squirrels frolic under the big magnolia tree.

With drinks in hand, the members rejoined Ginger. Ginger began, "today's topic is mindfulness and how we can use it to not only mitigate stress but to also make our day as enjoyable as possible. Mindfulness is more of a lifestyle approach than a technique you may use only occasionally." Ginger explained how you are creating thoughts all of the time and that we have a choice on how we frame our internal world. "We all have a universal desire to feel peaceful and happy. Mindfulness provides a method for us to feel greater joy. In its most raw form, mindfulness is about having nonjudgmental awareness of each moment. A simple task, you may think, but it is much harder to implement and use in our lives. A typical mind plays ping pong with present, past and future thinking. The mind darts from dwelling on the past to worrying about the future with little thought in the present. Mindfulness is a way to train the mind to be in the present, the only time in which we have any control. The past is past. The future has not arrived yet. However, this moment contains the jewel of contentment because we have a choice on how we are going to experience this moment. Realizing you always have a choice as to how you will respond in this moment is empowering. You may be wondering how this can help you. Grab your journals and turn your attention to what causes you stress. Consider the challenges you are currently facing and briefly jot them down." Ginger paused to give the members a chance to log their stressors. "Now write down your response to this question: what are you telling yourself about these stressors? In other words, what is going through your mind when you think about each response? Read each stress item, pause and listen to what comes to your mind," said Ginger.

After a few minutes, Ginger inquired, "what did you notice?"

Ann responded, "my thoughts went to asking why a lot. Why did this happen? Why am I in this situation?"

"Mine did too," Stephanie said.

Ginger responded, "and how does this line of thinking help you?"

Ann exclaimed, "wow! It doesn't! I just keep thinking about the same thing over and over."

Jerry jumped in and said, "I keep asking myself how I am going to do all of this without Mary. I am guessing this line of questioning doesn't help either."

"I keep asking myself whether or not I am doing the right thing," said Rayna. Realizing Miles had not contributed, she took it upon herself to ask him, "can you relate to any of this Miles?"

Miles looked back at Rayna and said, "I pretty much relate to all of it. I second guess my decisions a lot."

Ginger explained, "thoughts can often mimic a hamster running on a wheel. The mind jumps on the wheel of problems and keeps going and going but not getting anywhere! That is one of the main ways you can get trapped in problems instead of solutions. You get up and think about all the problems you are having. Most of your mental energy is spent ruminating on the problem instead of focusing on possible solutions. Telling yourself you can't handle the situation, or this is all too much are common negative thinking patterns. Telling yourself messages that you can't manage it is disempowering. These thoughts lead to mental fatigue."

"Another mental trap is fighting what is, rejecting what we are currently experiencing. Imagine standing waist high in the ocean. You see a big powerful wave approaching, and you try with all your might to hold back the oncoming wave. How well does that work?"

Stephanie said, "Oh," while Ginger noticed acknowledgement and recognition amongst the members' faces as they processed what they just heard.

Ginger said, "you most likely got knocked under the water and felt the push and pull of the current jostle you around a bit. Fighting the current taxes your muscles and strains your breath. You become exhausted fighting the reality of the wave." Ginger briefly paused for emphasis before she began again.

"There is another way. What if you accepted the wave coming, repositioned your body and rode the wave to the shore? No struggle necessary. No extra energy is expended. Your energy is preserved. Not only that, but once you have reached the shore you can look back at the ocean with a sense of triumph. The wave didn't take you. By succumbing to and accepting the wave, you harnessed your ability to use the resources at hand to carry you to shore. You probably agree this is the better approach. In the first scenario, you rejected the wave. You tried to control it by stopping it from doing what it naturally does. In the second situation, you accepted and prepared for the wave. You positioned yourself in the best stance to ride the wave. You worked with the wave to accomplish staying afloat. What in your life are you not accepting? What would happen if you decided to ride the wave instead?" The members sat their quietly lost in thought to this rhetorical question.

Ginger added, "unproductive thinking patterns often repeat themselves without offering any viable solutions. All these negative thinking patterns create stress. Stress is the internal reactions to an external situation. In other words, it is the story about the challenge that plays out in your mind. Your personal story affects your reaction. Your mental dialogue determines whether you will freeze, deny, persevere or rise through any difficult situation."

Members were attentive as they listened to Ginger. Stephanie and Ann took notes. Rayna tapped her pen on her leg as she briefly glanced out the window lost in her own thoughts. Miles nervously tapped his foot on the floor. Jerry appeared quite comfortable in group settings, probably from his many years of leading teams.

Jerry offered, "If we had to put them in a category, these types of thoughts you describe would be on the do not list when tackling new challenges? And yet, these are typical thought responses when stressed?"

"Yes, and these are only a few examples. You don't need to know all of them because you will learn how to recognize and weed them out," Ginger replied.

"Gotcha," Jerry said.

"Consider your mind a garden and you are learning how to pluck the weeds so that your garden will cultivate healthy, productive thoughts," said Ginger. She continued, "you are not your thoughts. Thoughts pop into your mind for various reasons. Thoughts can be random; they can be spontaneous, or they can be chosen. Thoughts are simply thoughts that come and go. It is when you react to random negative thoughts that contributes to distressing emotions."

"Can you give us an example?" asked Stephanie with pen in hand.

"Certainly," Ginger stated. "Have you ever felt guilty after making a quick judgement about someone you see at the store? The guilt comes from 'attaching' to the initial response and then feeling the reaction of guilt. You mentally beat yourself up for judging someone. You reacted to the thought and felt guilt."

Stephanie nodded in understanding. Ginger continued. "Mindfulness is about being aware of your thoughts and reactions in the moment without judgement. You cannot be kind and judgmental of yourself at the same time. When you release judgement of yourself and others, you are practicing kindness. To close today's session, I will guide you through a mindfulness practice that is simple, quick and easy to use."

Ginger walked them through the following mindfulness exercise; they would practice later at home and record their experiences in their journals.

Cindy C. Baker

5 Minute Mindfulness Activity

(To access your free audio version of the following mindfulness activity, go to www.rockinlifefromhome.com)

Assume a comfortable position and close your eyes. Rest your hands on your abdomen and feel your belly rise and fall with each breath. Notice any sensations in your body you may be feeling. Notice how the air feels through your nose as you inhale and exhale. Feel your chest and shoulders move with your breath. Take in the sounds around you. Notice the temperature in the room. Bring your awareness to your breath once more. Say silently in your mind, "breathing in and breathing out." Notice the rhythm and the connection between breath and body.

Most likely, your mind will stray from your focus. When you notice this, simply acknowledge your thoughts or feelings by stating silently "thinking, thinking, thinking now breathe," bringing your mind back to the breath. If you notice a feeling, again simply note it by saying silently "feeling, feeling, feeling, now breathe." Continue to guide your mind back to your breath and this present moment.

Go to www.rockinlifefromhome.com to download signs you can print and use throughout your house to prompt you to practice mindfulness. You can practice mindfulness while you cook, clean the house, brush your teeth, at a red light, the possibilities are endless. Simply take a couple of breaths and bring your attention to what you are doing in the present moment.

Week 2 Information Packet

Mindfulness in Action

Following through with your intentions is an important element in coping with change. When used consistently over time these new behaviors will form new habits. If you find yourself struggling to stay on task in the program, you may consider scheduling an individual coaching session to provide support and act as an accountability partner.

Mindfulness is about being aware of your thoughts, feelings, and behaviors in the present moment. Mindfulness is a practical application you can use in your life right away to help you gain tremendous insight and to help you manage stress. Mindfulness lays the groundwork to be able to recognize stress-based thoughts. The next step is being able to choose thoughts that are more productive and supportive.

Everyone in the family can benefit from practicing mindfulness. It provides an opportunity to pause, reflect and choose your responses. It is a gift to be able to pass this along to your kids.

Practice recognizing and dismissing negative thoughts. You cannot stop thoughts from popping into your mind but you can choose to ignore them and instead choose thoughts that will support and motivate you.

Common Negative Thinking Traps

I can't handle it. (I can't take it anymore.)

It is too hard.

I will never have (or be, or get) …

It always happens to me.

Why? (does this happen)

It will never get better. (It will never change)

This shouldn't be happening.

Replacing Negative Thoughts

When you catch your mind thinking negatively replace them with one (or more) of the following, helpful thoughts.

- I can handle this.
- Even though I feel stressed, I am learning new ways to help myself.
- I choose to be kind to myself and think in helpful ways.
- I am able.
- I am competent.
- I can do this!
- I will grow and learn from this situation.
- I will focus on what I can control versus what I cannot control.
- I accept this present situation and I will make the most out of this challenge.

Mindfulness Tips

Although there are many ways in which to practice mindfulness, there are common threads in all of them.

- Mindfulness meditation is a daily practice to daily ground and center yourself. It is not a goal to complete but a way of living that will enhance the quality of your life.
- It doesn't matter how many times you have to gently guide (keyword being gently) your mind back to the present. Remember this is not a contest – no judging allowed.
- Your practice may look and feel differently from one day to the next. Again, it is about the acceptance of whatever you are experiencing, observing and releasing – thoughts, judgements and expectations.

Benefits of Mindfulness Meditation

May be helpful with:

- decreasing stress
- regulating emotions
- managing your reactions
- calming your mind and body
- prompting relaxation
- feeling more centered for the day
- slowing down rapid thoughts
- releasing worry thoughts

CHAPTER 3
Session #3
Communication & Time Management

"Welcome back!" Ginger announced as the group filed in and took their regular seats.

Carrying a plate wrapped in cellophane, Rayna asked, "is it okay that I brought homemade chocolate chip cookies to share with everyone? My kids and I made them yesterday. I don't like to keep too many sweets lying around. I tend to have a bit of a sweet tooth and once I start eating them it is hard for me to stop!"

Ginger responded, "what a nice gesture. It is perfectly okay. Thank you." Jerry and Stephanie each grabbed a gooey cookie right away.

Ginger started off the session by saying, "last week you were introduced to the power of mindfulness and was given a homework assignment to practice it daily. Briefly tell me what that was like for you."

Ann said, "I found myself using it all throughout the day. I didn't realize how worked up I can get over the smallest of things. I even used it with my ten-year-old, Bobby. He got mad because I wouldn't let him sleep over at this friend's house because we were getting up early the next day to visit family. He started back-talking me and stomping his feet. I saw the info packet on the table and decided to teach him the mindfulness technique. I asked him to pause and think about how he was acting. We took a few deep breaths together. Then I asked him to communicate in a more respectful way. And it worked too! After a few minutes, he quit stomping his feet and was able to verbalize how he felt."

"That is terrific," said Ginger.

"You have motivated me to try it with my kids, Ann!" said Rayna.

Jerry jumped into the conversation next. "I ended up not only using it in the morning and at bedtime as you suggested, but also with work. I have a pretty demanding job and I felt myself losing my temper with one of our subcontractors. He wasn't doing a good enough job and he kept giving me excuse after excuse as to why the job wasn't finished. I wanted to fire him right then and there, but instead I ended the Zoom meeting early and rescheduled another meeting for the next morning. I practiced the mindfulness meditation to cool off. Afterwards, I found that I could think more clearly and come up with a solid plan to prepare for the next meeting."

Animatedly Ann said, "Ooh, you just gave me an idea. I can teach this to my team, and it can help them too! I am going to make a note of it right now," grabbing her journal.

Stephanie interjected, "I adore my child, Bethany, but she is also driving me crazy! She is at that terrible two-year-old phase where she throws her toys when she gets mad. This morning, she tried to bite me! Needless to say, she is trying my patience. I found myself doing a lot of breathing! Well, we are always breathing but you know what I mean. I was so happy to get out of the house to come to group today. I am with her non-stop except for these meetings. It gives me some grown up time."

"She will grow out of that phase soon. It gets better," Rayna said soothingly.

"I hope so," replied Stephanie.

Concerned over Mile's lack of participation, Rayna turned and asked him, "How was your week, Miles?"

"It was okay, I guess. I started taking lunch and afternoon breaks like we talked about. That helps. It gives more structure to my day. My wife is still interrupting me though. I have been using the mindfulness practice in the mornings before I start work though, and that has helped me get focused for the day."

Rayna said, "my days are so hectic I barely have time to go to the bathroom, let alone meditate!" The group snickered along with her and she continued. "I often lie awake in bed running through my day again and thinking about all the things I need to do for the next day. It is the only quiet time I get to myself. I practiced at night to settle my mind before going to sleep. I had to bring my mind back to my breath a lot. I noticed after the first few nights it did help me relax and fall asleep more quickly than usual."

"I am glad you found it helpful," Ginger said. "It is important to continue to practice so that it will become second nature to you. Everything in these sessions are designed to be building blocks, incorporating each lesson into your life that will help you rock life from home. "

As Ginger passed out this week's education packet, Ann seized the opportunity to grab a cookie. "These are so yummy, Rayna," Ann said.

Rayna responded, "I am glad you like them. We love to bake in our house as you can see." Rayna smiled as she patted her tummy.

As the members shuffled through their handouts, Ginger said, "today we are going to explore communication and time management strategies. The way homes are used has evolved over time and they now serve as multi-functional spaces. Homes serve as businesses, multi-generational living, work offices, and learning environments in addition to places for spending quality family time together. Homes work hard to accommodate our varying needs. Just as open living/dining/kitchen spaces have a central flow to them, so does your day. Proper time management is essential to organize your work and home lives. You face specific demands on your time as you combine work and parenting obligations. Even though Rayna is the only one homeschooling a child, the rest of you still must manage homework and after school activities. Plus, Stephanie has her little one all day. After looking over the material, we will take a break so you can grab something to drink and stretch your legs."

Rayna, Jerry, and Ann headed straight for the coffee while Stephanie called home to check on her daughter, Bethany, who had been up in the middle of the night cutting a new tooth. Miles grabbed one of the few cookies left on the plate, and surprisingly, instead of going outside, he walked up to Rayna and thanked her for the cookies. Rayna smiled and patted his shoulders in return. After checking on Bethany, Stephanie made a cup of hot steaming tea and joined the others. Clearly, the members were feeling more comfortable around each other.

Regrouping once again, Ginger asked the group to jot down in their journal the biggest challenges they are currently facing at home. She said, "I would like each one of you to comment on the challenges you wrote down."

Ann leaped at the opportunity to talk. "Ya'll know by now that I love people and I love to talk. So, for me, it has been hard working in seclusion. Not only that but managing the afternoons; herding my kids through snack time and completing homework assignments while I am trying to work has been stressful. I tend to get a bit snippy with them to be honest. I always feel bad afterwards."

Stephanie empathized, "I totally feel you. It is hard going back and forth between parenting and working. I feel like my brain is in a ping pong match and my brain is losing! Because Bethany is so young, I often have her in the same room with me while I am designing my jewelry and handling all the administrative parts of my business."

Rayna interjected by saying, "if you recall, I put Elijah's computer in my office. It is working rather well so far. I can make sure he is doing the work instead of daydreaming and doodling like he was in school. I did get the online tutor." She paused as she gathered her thoughts before continuing further. "There is a noise factor though. I must be available anytime for phone and video meetings. Sometimes they pop up and aren't scheduled in advance. My boss calls me several times a day about something. I swear that man would lose his head if it wasn't attached! He called me last Friday to ask me the date of his last out-of-town conference he attended! The man has a calendar. He could have looked it up himself; but no, he had to call me. I know I am his assistant but goodness some things he could do himself. I am like his work wife! Well, I digressed. The other day I didn't answer when my boss called because Elijah was online with his tutor. How professional would that have sounded? He would have heard voices and wondered if I was having a party or something during work hours." Rayna shook her head in frustration.

Part of the purpose of the group is to allow a place to openly vent about their stressors and in return receive support and feedback. Stephanie tentatively suggested putting Elijah's computer desk on wheels so he can move it into another room for his tutoring sessions so that Rayna's work wouldn't be interrupted. Rayna pondered the notion and responded with, "That is a really good idea. I don't know why I didn't think of that. Maybe my neighbor can help. He is known around the neighborhood as 'Mr. Fixit.' He is a retired builder who is always offering to help everybody. He fixed my leaky sink once and refused to take a penny from me. Of course I didn't feel right about it so me and the kids made him homemade macaroni and cheese as a thank you." It looked like Rayna was about to say something then paused, looking embarrassed. She said, "There is one more noise problem. You are going to have a good laugh about this. You see...it's my dog. I love her to death but she is as yappy as they come! She is this little sable colored Pomeranian fur ball. She is the sweetest thing, but she barks at everything. Once when I was on the phone with a vendor, the mailman knocked on the door and she went ballistic. I couldn't hear a thing that man was telling me! It was outright embarrassing, let alone highly unprofessional. I don't know what to do about her."

Ginger smiled and responded, "pets are a part of the family and apply to boundaries as well. Before we start talking about possible solutions, though, I would like to hear from the rest of the group."

Jerry cleared his throat and began, "It feels good to know that I am not the only one struggling with my schedule. And you all have been doing it a lot longer than I have. I am spending almost every afternoon driving my kids to and from their activities. It's really impacting my work. I am just not as accessible late in the day like I need to be."

Recognizing he was last, Miles said, "my biggest problem is my wife interrupting me. She is just so excited to share what our son is doing. There are so many milestones at this age. He is only six months old."

Rayna asked, "what do you do when your wife interrupts you?"

"I remind her I am working. She apologizes and leaves the room," Miles said.

Knowing that everyone now had had a turn, all eyes expectantly roamed to Ginger. Reassuring the group, she said, "before the end of session, you will be leaving with steps you can take to help your households run more smoothly. However, first I will go over a few key concepts for success at home. You read over your packet on today's topic, boundary setting. Each one of the challenges you mentioned has to do with time management and boundary setting. As we discuss these concepts more fully, think about how you can apply the material in your lives."

"Setting healthy boundaries starts with using assertive communication. You want to be able to express your needs, wants and desires without infringing upon the rights of other family members. To do this, use 'I' statements when talking. Do not use any derogatory or blaming language. Stick to the present issue only. Refer to the handout provided (Packet #3) and encourage your whole family to start using this communication style."

She continued. "Effective communication is open and honest. It is important first to be honest with yourself as to what you need, so that you can adequately express your ideas to your family. It takes courage to practice assertiveness and release any fears that may arise from the thought of you voicing your needs. It is easy to fall into the trap of assuming how another will respond. Use mindfulness to release any assumptions, doubts or fears."

Stephanie asked, "do you mean thoughts that your idea won't work? Does that count too?"

"Precisely," Ginger answered. "Often we shoot down a viable solution or option because our minds will fill in the details as to why something won't work. That is a great example, Stephanie. It is important to recognize them as unhelpful thought processes and reach for more supportive thoughts that are in alignment with our intentions. There is more information on this in your packets as well."

Ginger continued, "because you are wearing multiple hats at once, good time management is imperative in reducing stress and accomplishing your 'to do' lists. Consider 'chunking down' your time by breaking up your day into more manageable pieces. Instead of looking at the whole day in its entirety, compartmentalize your day into sections so that you can more easily divide your tasks. You will most likely find your agenda easier to manage. Stephanie, you may find this particularly helpful when structuring your workday. Schedule fewer intensive tasks when Bethany is awake while reserving tasks that require more focus during her naptimes or in the evenings when your husband is available." Stephanie nodded and jotted something in her journal.

Addressing the whole group Ginger said, "also keep in mind, spending quality time with family over quantity. Spending fifteen to thirty minutes with your kids before you start work can help them transition to you working as well. The same applies to kids when they get home from school. They want your attention and want to talk about their day. This can be a precious time to reconnect with them after being apart for several hours."

Ann interjected, "I just had an idea. When my kids get home, I usually tell them to go get a snack and start their homework so I can get back to work as quickly as possible. I didn't realize I was missing out on a good opportunity to bond with my kids. After hearing what you said, I could take a late lunch so that they could join me for a snack when they get off the bus. Since it would be my official lunch time, I wouldn't feel so pressured to get back to work right away. Plus, it would be great not having to eat alone."

"That sounds like a good plan," Rayna added. "Even though Elijah is home with me, we have been eating lunch at different times. Starting tomorrow, we are having lunch together," Rayna said with a smile. "Now if only I could figure out what to do with my yappy dog!" Rayna exclaimed.

Stephanie responded, "Before Bethany was born my pug, Daisy, slept in the bed with us. When I got pregnant, I started crate training her so I could put her in there at night and anytime I couldn't watch her around our newborn. I found a trainer online that posts a bunch of free tutorials on YouTube that really helped. I can give you his name if you would like."

"That would be terrific; thank you, Stephanie!" Rayna replied.

Taking advantage of the momentary silence, Ginger interjected, "part of self-care is knowing when to ask for help. It is typically assumed that when you ask for help you are viewed as weak. However, that is not true at all. Strong people do not suffer in silence. Strong people reach out and ask for assistance. Think about it this way. Asking friends or family members for help allows them an opportunity to give and it feels good to help others. You are allowing people who care about you a chance to connect and support you. By reaching out you feel less alone."

Jerry said, "Wow, you said exactly what I needed to hear. My wife has been telling me for weeks to contact the parents of the kids that are involved in the same after school activities as ours to set up a carpool, but I was pigheaded. She said they would be more than happy to help out so I could get more work done. I didn't want to admit I needed help. It felt like I wasn't being a man if I couldn't take care of it all. It's funny. Looking back, it seems I chose to be stressed out instead of asking for help and getting some relief."

Looking surprised Jerry said, "the things we do to ourselves. Ya know what? My situation hasn't changed a bit. My wife is still out of town. I am still home juggling everything, but something in me has shifted. I feel less weighted down. I guess the way I am approaching the situation has changed."

Ginger commented, "I agree. What you are telling yourself about your situation has changed. In other words, an internal change has occurred. You have let go of thoughts, such as being perceived as weak if you asked for help, that were contributing to your stress. And as you let this thought go, your mind is open to consider the option of carpooling to manage your day. You are now able to entertain new solutions that you were unable to previously."

Jerry replied, "yea, it feels good too; like a new door is open I can choose to walk through."

Looking at Miles, Ginger inquired, "how often is your wife coming into the office interrupting you?"

"Um, about three times a day," Miles answered.

"Okay, what is it about these interruptions that bothers you the most?" asked Ginger.

Miles answered, "I guess I have a hard time focusing and I don't want to be bothered. It has always irritated me when people try to talk to me when I am working. It was like that in college too. I would get upset if people interrupted me while I was studying." Miles was silent as he considered what he just said. "Hmm, it sounds like I am the one with the problem, not her" Miles said as he fidgeted with his shoelaces. "What can I do about this?" he asked.

Ginger stated, "it sounds like you tell yourself it is a bother to be interrupted, which in turn causes the frustrated feelings." Ginger waited for a response.

Miles answered, "I guess so. I never thought of it that way."

"What may benefit you in this case is a shift in mindset." Ginger continued, "interpret the interruptions as something different. You could tell yourself instead that is normal to be occasionally interrupted. It is okay to take a few breaths to help you refocus on your work. Allow room in your mind for brief interruptions remembering that mindfulness practice is about welcoming the present moment without judgement of yourself or others. In the simplest of terms, change the way you are looking at the situation so that it no longer causes undue stress." Miles nodded his head in agreement.

Addressing the group again Ginger said, "the beauty of the mindfulness pause is it allows you time to think through and respond the way you want versus being reactive. I like to remind myself to be kind when I am using the mindfulness pause. It totally changes the way I look at the situation and how I respond in the moment. As I breathe in, I contemplate what would be the kind response - for myself and any others involved. This also gives me an opportunity to check my tone, my facial expressions and body language."

A silent lull penetrated the air, taking the last few comments in. Looking surprised, Rayna said, "whoa, I can see how that would be really challenging to do but so beneficial if I can remember to do that when I am getting frustrated with the kids. Last night the kids were supposed to clean up the dinner plates and put them in the dishwasher. I walked in the kitchen this morning and saw all the dishes piled in the sink. Food stuck on them like cement! I stormed right into their rooms, woke them up early fussing at them, and made them clean everything up before school. Needless to say, it was not an enjoyable morning. If I had used the mindfulness pause, I still would have had them clean up, but I wouldn't have been so angry about it. I probably would have approached the situation differently."

Contributing Ann said, "it just dawned on me how much I respond reactively instead of proactively like you mentioned earlier, Ginger. To me, this approach is a much better way to live. I can see myself controlling my emotions better. I am sure my husband would appreciate that too!" Ann chuckled.

Ginger smiled and said, "Yes, it can be quite empowering. I call it Kind Connect Mindfulness. The pause acts as a place holder as you focus on using kindness to guide your response. Using this technique allows you to tap into your prefrontal cortex (the forehead area) where you engage in higher thinking processes and problem solving. Furthermore, it helps you switch from your emotional center, which can react quickly, to thinking before reacting."

Wrapping up today's session, Ginger said, "each one of you now has a plan to address the challenges you spoke about today. Going forward, it is important to use the education on boundaries and apply it to your individual challenges. Assess your needs and determine how you can leverage boundary setting at home. Please take a few minutes and write down your plan in your journal. Use your journal to log-in your successes in boundary setting and the techniques you used that you find helpful. Enjoy the rest of your week, and I will see you for our final session next Monday."

Cindy C. Baker

Week 3 Information Packet

Communication and Time Management

There are many benefits that arise from working from home. New situations give you an opportunity to transform challenges into opportunities. It gives you a forum to practice new approaches. It gives you a chance to become closer as a family. It also forces you to use your creativity in re-designing your workday.

Just like spring cleaning provides an opportunity for reflection to see what you want to keep and what you want to get rid of, working from home is an evaluation period to see what works and what doesn't work. You can tweak and change what is not working and adopt new, productive methods. Approach your day as an experiment using assertive communication and time management strategies to optimize your day.

Effective Communication for the Whole Family

Strive to:

- Use assertive communication – express your thoughts, feelings, and actions without trying to take away someone else's rights.
- Stick to the present issue only
- Maintain an open mind
- Listen more than you speak
- Use "I" statements (I feel…I think…I would like to…)
- Check in with the other person to make sure you understand what he/she is saying by summarizing what you just heard (What I hear you saying is…is this right?) Fully allow the other person to respond by either saying yes or clarifying.
- Briefly discuss the problem, then switch gears and focus on possible solutions.
- Take timeouts (5-10 minutes) as needed to calm down. When too emotional, you cannot focus on solutions.
- Be honest
- Practice Kind Connect Mindfulness (pause, breathe, filter response through being kind to yourself and others)
- Remember that each of you has your own perceptions, history, and life experience.
- Remind yourself in the moment that this is your family and you love them.

Avoid:

- Bringing up past issues
- Projecting issue into the future
- Assuming how another will respond
- Using labels, name calling, finger pointing, unpleasant language
- Getting into each other's faces, remain a respectful distance
- Keep score or try to win (this is not a contest - the goal is to seek understanding, support, and love from one another).

Download the communications chart at www.rockinlifefromhome.com.

Time Management Success

- Keep your daily list to a max of 10 items, max of 5 if they are big, time consuming chores.
- Prioritize your list – rate the list from 1 to 10, 10 being the highest priority. Then re-rank your list accordingly.
- Write your list either the night before or first thing in the morning, whichever works best for you.
- Tasks you do not accomplish become the priority for the next day.
- Create a flexible weekly schedule. Pencil in errands such as grocery shopping so you have a set day to accomplish these chores. Establish daily meal and exercise plans so you can put your energy elsewhere. Having structure ensures the necessary plans get carried out each week without trying to "fit" them in.
- "Chunk" your time down into smaller units, such as morning, afternoon, and evening. It is easier to focus on bitesize portions. Plus, it is less daunting to look at part of the day versus the entire day's agenda.
- Be realistic about what you can reasonably accomplish.
- Say "no" to outside requests whenever you have enough on your plate and when your energy is depleted. (Give yourself permission to say no and release any accompanying thoughts of guilt).

- Ask for help when needed. Do not try to be superman or superwoman. Asking for help allows others to feel good giving back to you.
- Practice mindfulness to welcome the present as it births each new moment (enjoy the process).

CHAPTER 4
Final Group Session #4
Boundary Setting and Beyond

Monday came quickly, dark clouds cast a gloomy haze and dropped rain pellets from the sky as the members entered the office with umbrellas in hand. Ginger greeted everyone as she quickly shuffled papers around attempting to catch up on her paperwork. "There is a fresh pot of coffee available; help yourself," said Ginger.

The aroma permeated the air and drew Ann and Jerry straight towards the kitchenette. Stephanie joined them once she put down her purse, this time a big hot pink floral bag. "I need caffeine!" Stephanie said. "If only there were a 24-ounce super-sized mug around here," she groaned.

"Tough night?" asked Rayna as she approached.

"I stayed up late cleaning my house," Stephanie replied.

"I thought you were going to say you had an exciting night out on the town with your girlfriends or something more interesting than cleaning your house," Rayna teased.

"I know, right? I wish," said Stephanie. "I didn't want to miss out on family time, so I put off cleaning the house until after my husband and Bethany went to sleep. It was not one of my better decisions," a groggy, frazzled Stephanie replied.

Joining the conversation, Jerry said, "my teenage kids always laugh at me because I can't stay awake past ten. We can be in the middle of the action-packed big box office hit movie and they will catch me snoring away!" He laughed as they walked to the sitting area where Miles and Ginger were waiting.

Looking rather uncomfortable, Miles for the first time initiated the conversation. "I would like to go first if that is okay." Everyone looked shocked and pleased at the same time.

"Of course, go ahead Miles," encouraged Ginger.

"I took what you said last week to heart. It wasn't easy. I did have a talk with my wife. She said she understood. Even though my wife and I did have a talk, she still comes into the office, but at least it is not as much.as it was before. I placed a blue sticky note on my computer to remind me to pause before reacting to my wife when she interrupted me. I noticed I didn't get as tense as I usually do. It took me a few minutes to refocus on my work, but I told myself that it was okay and that I could take as much time as I needed. It was concerted effort, but I was able to manage it better. So, thank you for the advice."

"You are welcome," Ginger answered, "I am glad you found it helpful. And remember, the more you practice, the easier it will become. In time you won't have to concentrate so hard on it because it will feel like second nature."

Miles smiled and replied, "I will do my best."

Next, Ann took the floor. "Last week was a much better week for me. I switched my lunch to 2:30 when the kids get off the bus. That made a huge difference in my day. They have a snack while I eat lunch. We talk about how their day was at school. After my lunch hour, the kids are ready to go play. Come to think about it, they interrupted me a lot less than they had been doing. I noticed I am more relaxed too and found myself looking forward to them getting home."

"That is terrific, Ann," Rayna said encouragingly. "I wish my dog was that easy! Stephanie, I watched the training videos you advised. I got a crate and everything. She does not like it one little bit. She is spoiled rotten! She yaps and yaps and yaps! I am not giving up though. I am determined to win out on this one. It doesn't help that Elijah sneaks her out when I am not looking. I caught him the other day. She was sitting on his lap during his tutoring session! My kids sure do love that dog."

Stephanie giggled, "It just takes some time…and consistency. Make sure Elijah only takes her out of the cage when she is quiet. Otherwise, it teaches her barking gets her out of the cage."

"That makes perfect sense. I will tell Elijah today when I get home," Rayna said.

Jerry placed his coffee cup on the table and said, "I went home after our meeting last week and called a couple of parents my wife had suggested right away. I didn't give myself a chance to talk myself out of it. They were more than willing to help out. They said they would take care of all the carpooling but that didn't feel right. We came to an agreement, however, that I feel pretty good about. I am in charge of carpooling Wednesdays and Fridays. Fridays are usually pretty light for me. Many of my meetings are at the beginning of the week so now I don't have to worry about missing another appointment."

"How is your wife and her mother doing?" inquired Rayna.

"My mother in law is doing well. She is up and moving around some. I have been sharing what we talk about in group with my wife and it has been helping her manage her stress better too. If all continues to go well, it looks like Mary will be home in a few weeks."

"I bet she will be so happy to be back home," Rayna said.

"We both will," Jerry said.

Stephanie looked around at the members. "It looks like I am the last to go this time," Stephanie noticed. "Ugh, I don't think I did as well as the rest of you."

"This isn't a contest, Stephanie," Rayna said. "No one is judging you except you."

Nodding her head, Stephanie exclaimed, "you're right; I am! I try so hard and it doesn't work out like it is supposed to. I prioritized my 'to do' lists the night before. It was tough trying to list only ten items. I kept wanting to add more. Ten doesn't seem like enough. Anyway, I had it planned to create some new pieces while Bethany slept. But three days last week she skipped her nap altogether! I cannot make jewelry with her around. I don't want her getting the little pieces in her mouth. Instead I have been staying up late every night making jewelry except for last night when I cleaned my house. You should have seen it. It looked like a tornado went through it. Toys everywhere, baskets of laundry that needed folding and don't get me started on the dust." Stephanie sighed and dropped her shoulders. Clearly, she was struggling, and she was also exhausted.

"It seems Stephanie is putting a lot of pressure on herself. Where is this pressure coming from?" Ginger gently asked.

"Me," Stephanie replied. "My husband keeps telling me the house looks fine. I hate feeling this overwhelmed…and tired. What can I do?"

"Considering what you strive to accomplish in a day, ask yourself 'what will matter the most in 5 years?'" advised Ginger.

Stephanie thought for a moment with a puzzled look on her face. She answered, "Bethany and my work are what will matter the most in five years. So I guess, being a parent, raising my child to the best of my ability, and growing as an entrepreneur and artist."

"Exactly, focus your time and energy on what matters the most. Give yourself more flexibility in the other areas. When you start feeling stressed, use this question to help you determine where to place your time. Be sure to include taking care of yourself in your answer as well. Sacrificing sleep may help you catch up on tasks, but it can physically and emotionally run you down. Practice telling yourself that you don't have to be perfect nor does the house have to look perfect. You may have to skip family time once or twice a week to make your jewelry but on the bright side it also allows for special father/daughter bonding time too" Ginger replied.

Stephanie smiled and relaxed as if a burden was lifted off of her. "I don't know why I didn't think of that before! It would be good for them to have some one-on-one time, thank you," said Stephanie. Ginger smiled and nodded to Stephanie.

Addressing the group, Ginger said, "when you are struggling with designing a solution to challenges, imagine looking at the problem from a distance. Just like the zoom out button on a camera, zooming out of the problem allows you to gain perspective and insight by seeing the entire picture. Look for solutions and opportunities for growth. This will help you when you are managing working and parenting roles at the same time."

Ginger passed the last information packet out to the group. While the members took a few minutes to look it over, Ginger grabbed a bright yellow folder from her large wooden desk. Ginger returned to her seat and waited for everyone to signal they were done by looking up at the group.

Ginger cleared her throat and said, "you all have done a tremendous job over the past few weeks of managing your stress better and adopting new habits that are in alignment with your goals. Give yourselves a big pat on the back!" The group laughed as they patted themselves.

Ginger smiled and continued, "It is hard for your mind to focus on thriving when you are facing life challenges. Stress and unwanted circumstances drive you to focus on surviving, getting through the day. When you are overwhelmed, trying to focus on enriching your life is unrealistic. Basic survival needs must be met first. You don't normally catapult from surviving to thriving in one day. It is a process that takes time. Over the last three sessions you learned how to manage your circumstances better. It is time to focus on thriving. Today, we are looking at setting boundaries and ways to enhance the family unit. We could take days and days to explore this one topic, it is so big. Instead, this will be an overview on things you can implement right away to make profound, significant changes at home."

Ginger advised the group to take a few minutes to imagine their ideal home life and describe in their journals how they see themselves interacting with their families during the day. Next, they were to describe the biggest difference between their home life now and their ideal home life. Ginger suggested they take a break after the assignment.

Ann and Jerry made their way to the coffee pot first. Jerry shared how his daughter's dance recital went last night. "I am so proud of her. She has so much passion for dance and it really comes out in her performance," he told Ann.

"It is nice to know what you want to do at such a young age," Ann commented.

Overhearing their conversation, Rayna said, "I am thirty-eight and I still don't know what I want to be when I grow up!" Rayna turned to Miles as he waited in the coffee line and asked, "Miles, did you always want to work with technology?"

"I always tinkered with computers; even in elementary school I was coding programs," Miles replied.

"It saves a lot of time and energy if you know your career path at a young age," Rayna said.

Walking up, Stephanie said, "Tell me about it! I have had so many different kinds of jobs. Waitress, retailer, nanny, you name it and I have done it. I even sold cell phones! School wasn't really my thing. I worked odd jobs all throughout school. I moved out of my family's house when I graduated high school and into my own apartment with a couple of friends. It wasn't until I took a jewelry making course at the community center that I discovered my passion. It really helped unleash the creativity that I didn't know I was craving. Everything seemed to fit. Even though I haven't been designing jewelry for long, it just feels right." Looking at Rayna, Stephanie said, "You could schedule a one-on-one coaching appointment with Ginger. I read on her website she offers career coaching." Rayna replied, "That might work. I will give it some thought."

Noticing that break time was up, they scurried back to their seats. Ginger asked, "What did you all notice about this activity?"

Ann said, "I realized I don't think too much about what I really want out of my relationships. I am more focused on getting everything done throughout the day. I am ashamed to admit it, but I place more attention on my work. I forgot to put in the time needed to make my home life thrive as well. Don't get me wrong, my husband and kids are terrific. I am blessed that they are all happy and healthy. I wrote in my journal that I want to create even deeper relationships with each of them. I realize one huge benefit from working at home is the special time I have been spending with the kids when they get home from school. I have never had that before. I feel more connected with them and I want the connection to grow even more."

"Thank you for being so open about how you are feeling," said Ginger.

Showing her support, Rayna said, "we all can learn from each other if we are brave enough to express what we think. And there is nothing to be ashamed about. It is hard keeping everything in balance. This simply gives you an opportunity to shift your priorities and spend some time building a tighter family. For me, I need to have more meaningful conversations with my kids. I want to know what they really want in their lives. I want to talk to them about their passions and dreams, not just about homework and chores."

Jerry joined in on the conversation. "It is easy to lose sight of what is most important. Being so driven to provide for my family has also come with a downside. I don't know my kids nearly as well as my wife does. They grow up so fast."

"I decided to stop taking myself so seriously! I think if I can lighten up, I will feel more relaxed, which will have a positive effect on my family," said Stephanie.

Miles chuckled softly and said, "I know I waited last to speak again." The members all shared a laugh together. Miles seemed much more at ease than he had been in the first couple of sessions. No longer going outside, Miles joined the others at breaktime. Now he was even making jokes about himself. "Like the rest of you, I too would like a closer relationship with my family. We are pretty good but there is room to make it even better."

Ginger said, "I think you all have done a great job diving deep into the question on what your ideal family relationships would look like. And some of you even began thinking of ways to enhance your relationships. This is no place for blame or guilt. There are many demands in your life and sometimes work needs more attention. Sometimes, extended family needs you. Sometimes, health challenges require you to redirect your focus to healing your body. Life balance is not about having all elements in your life balance equally. That is totally unrealistic. To me, life balance is about regularly reviewing areas in your life and shifting your attention where it is needed. In other words, life balance is fluid, it molds, shifts and changes along with the flow of life. Once a month or once a quarter, do a mini review of what areas are working well and what area or areas may need some attention."

Ginger continued, "Consider what you need to see happen to make it a successful workday. What does it look like? What support do you need from your family? Use your answers as a guide to construct your day." The members grabbed their journal to capture their responses.

A few minutes later, Ginger said, "I would like to share with you ideas on setting boundaries to help you manage your workday. Two biggest factors in helping your day flow well are using effective strategies with yourself and with your family. Creating best practices will provide the necessary structure needed for you to be able to mesh work and home life together more easily.

Let's start with your approach to work. It is extremely easy to get bogged down in work when your office is at home. There are no coworkers to encourage you to go home. There are no janitors prompting you to leave so they can do their job and clean your office. Plus, with the technology we have available today you are always reachable through phones, emails and chats at the sound of the click that can grab your attention. It is imperative that you shut down your "work brain" each day. Having an established routine can help you transition from work mode to off mode. Designate a time you will start and end your day and stick to it. Turn off all reminders on your phone on the evenings and weekends. Resist the urge to check your messages when you are not officially working. Develop a ritual when "leaving" the office. For example, you could take three deep breaths while saying silently, 'I now close the door to work, leaving all work thoughts behind me. I now enter free time to enjoy as I see fitting.' Transition with intention. When you rush from one activity to the next, you lose sight of intention. Taking deep breaths and bringing your mind to this moment give space to birth intentionality.

Now, let's talk about putting structure in place with your family. Plan your workday around spending quality time with your kids. Quality time will look differently depending upon the age of your children. Younger kids may enjoy you reading a book or coloring before you head into your office. You could spend that time talking with older kids, say tweens or teens. If you have an energetic child, schedule a physical activity first thing in the morning. Younger kids could play outside whereas teens may workout or go for a run in the neighborhood."

Rayna said, "Elijah always has lots of energy, which is one of the reasons why he kept getting into trouble at school. I usually have him start homeschooling right after breakfast. I will suggest he go for a run instead. He will probably love that!"

"That is a good idea," Stephanie added, "Bethany and I could do some mommy and me yoga in the mornings!"

"That sounds great," Ginger continued. "Please write your ideas in your journal so you won't forget them. Spending quality time can also be spent helping kids transition home after a school day or when getting up from naps. Personalize quality time to fit you and your family's individual needs."

"If you oversee schoolwork, either homeschool or homework, you may want to have them sit with you while you finish up your day. That way you are available to answer any questions and to make sure the work is being completed."

"Kids need time adjusting to you working from home. They are excited to have you home and will most likely want to interrupt you often. It will take some patience on your part to help them learn new routines. It is important to teach them to respect your worktime. Role model appropriate behavior by setting firm boundaries around your workday. Otherwise, you won't get much accomplished and you will be left with a good bit of frustration all around."

"Go over with them when they can and when they cannot talk to you. You can put a 'do not disturb' sign on your door when you have calls and meetings where you cannot be disrupted. You can use signal reminders such as a finger over your mouth to indicate no talking. If your kids are older you can give them a schedule that reflects needed private time. If appropriate, have the older kids look after the younger ones. Rayna, since your office doesn't have a door you could attach a string and a 'quiet please' sign in the entry way."

"Make sure they understand what constitutes a good reason to disrupt you. If there is a fire, yes; if you are out of popcorn, then no." The members chuckled softly.

"That reminds me," Ann said, "my little girl, Dee Dee, came into my office one day last week. She said, 'look mommy, isn't she pretty?' Using her baby doll clothes, she dressed up our dog in a pink tutu and put little barrettes in her hair. She looked like Chewbacca's girlfriend! I laughed so hard I snorted. It was so loud you would have thought I was hiding a pig in my office!"

Everyone shared a laugh together as they imagined what that must have looked like. After catching her breath Ann said, "Fortunately, I was not on the phone at the time."

After everyone settled back down, Ginger said, "reward your kid's positive behavior. Often, we tend to only speak up when they are doing something we don't like or want. However, reinforcing the actions you want to see in them not only encourages future positive behaviors it also helps kids build healthy self-esteem."

Ginger continued, "Rayna brought up an excellent point earlier about having meaningful conversations with her children. Schedule a family meeting to openly talk about what can make the work/school day flow better. Have each family member briefly state any problems. Encourage your family to focus more on the solutions and less on the challenges. Kids can be incredibly inciteful and come up with creative ways to overcome challenges when given the chance. Be sure to follow up with them to make sure everyone feels the solutions are working. A family is a team and a team supports each other for the greater good of the entire unit."

Jerry nodded and said, "I think that is a good way to look at family. At work I spend a lot of time listening to and motivating my sales team. I reward them when they meet their sales quota for the month, which in return keeps them engaged. When my wife returns home, I think we can have a discussion about how we as parents can be more encouraging and supportive to our kids as they are rapidly becoming young adults."

"Sounds terrific, Jerry," Ginger stated. Keeping an eye on the time, Ginger noted it was time to move on to the last activity.

Ginger said, "let's do one more journal activity." The members reached for their journals. Stephanie immediately began shuffling through the contents of her enormous bag. Miles reached under the chair for his while Rayna and Ann retrieved theirs from the coffee table. Jerry's was sitting on his lap with pen at the ready. Ginger instructed them to take a few minutes to write about what they have gotten out of this group and what has changed for them since day one.

"Who would like to go first?" asked Ginger once she saw everyone was done writing. Surprising everyone, Miles volunteered.

"I am pushing myself out of my comfort zone," he said with a smile. "It is not easy for me to speak in front of people, but I feel comfortable in this group. I was super stressed, more stressed than I let on at the first meeting. Maybe you could tell…I don't know. I learned to think about people, even myself, differently. I am less stressed now and that is a big deal to me."

"I am so glad you felt at ease with us, Miles," said Rayna.

"Me too," Miles replied. He looked satisfied with himself and more relaxed than ever.

"I was feeling so isolated when I signed up for the class," said Ann. "I had just relocated my office to home. I had to learn not only how to function working alone but also how to manage taking care of my kids in the afternoons, something else I wasn't used to either. It was a lot of change all at once. Like Miles, I was feeling pretty overwhelmed. I didn't know what to expect from this class but the idea kept popping into my mind, like a little voice was beckoning for me to register. I am definitely glad I listened to that little voice. This group gave me a place to express how I was feeling, and I felt supported because all of you were experiencing something similar. Instead of getting caught up in my emotions, I learned to strategize optimal solutions and make small, consistent changes."

Rayna speaking next said, "I mentioned at the beginning I was raised with the belief to keep my problems to myself. I will admit it was hard for me to come here. Fortunately, my desire to find a better way trumped this old family belief. I agree with Ann that being able to connect and feel supported has made a big difference. Being a single mom, I feel an overarching level of responsibility since I am the only parent my kids can rely on. I was in my own head too much. Participating in this group helped me realize I can make changes that will help reduce daily stress. Even small changes help more than I realized. Elijah is doing better academically too. I think the change was good for him," said Rayna.

"Yay!" said Stephanie, encouragingly. "I learned a lot coming here, but, I still have a long way to go!" She stopped short and looked surprised. "Oops!" Stephanie said after realizing she was being too hard on herself. Carefully reframing she said, "What I mean to say is I want to learn and grow even more. What can I say? I have caught the 'personal growth bug!'" She giggled. "That is probably my biggest take away from this class. I now know what I didn't know before. I now know I can take control over my destiny. Things don't just 'happen' to me. Life 'happens' to everyone. I can control the way I respond to things that happen to me. I can choose to be a stressed -out perfectionistic person or I can choose to be a calm, peaceful person. I can choose to be proactive or I can choose to be reactive. I guess you can say I feel more empowered."

"Well said, Stephanie!" Rayna said warmly.

"Thanks!" Stephanie replied with a smile.

Jerry, thinking logically and methodically, said, "two main learning points stand out for me. One is to ask for help whether I want to or not. When I hit a certain stress level, I am going to reach out for help both at work and at home. I have decided to cut back on my work hours. I will delegate more tasks to my team. I don't think I would have made this decision had I not taken this class. Secondly, I am going to spend more quality time with my family. I think my wife will enjoy that too."

Ginger said, "It sounds like each of you have had some profound and meaningful insights into your lives. I am happy that you have received benefit from the class. This was our final session together. Hopefully, you have not only acquired, but will continue to use, new tools, strategies, and coping skills to help you enjoy your life more. We also have a free once-a-month support group that you can attend. It is nice to have a friendship group that is focused on creating abundant, happy lives. I hope you will take advantage of this group and keep in touch with everyone here." She retrieved the green folder from under her chair. Ginger passed out Certificates of Completion to each member.

"It has been such a pleasure getting to know you and I wish each of you continued happiness, peace and joy."

Week 4 Information Packet

Boundary Setting and Beyond

Setting boundaries around work and family will help your day run more smoothly and effectively.

Tips for setting work boundaries:

- Stick to a regular work schedule.
- Establish a routine for transitioning from work mode to off mode.
- Once you leave the office, stay out of the office until the next official workday begins.
- Turn off alerts for your messages, emails, etc. so you are not tempted to check them during off time.

Tips for setting boundaries with family:

- Build in short bursts of quality time with children.
- Help children transition from one activity to the next (i.e., getting home from school, snack time, homework time, etc.)
- Have a family talk about expectations while you are working.
- Use do not disturb or quiet please signs to indicate when you are not to be disturbed.
- Reward positive behaviors.

Consider your ultimate work from home experience and write it down where you will frequently see it. Out of sight is out of mind. Placing them in a strategic location will ensure it gets your attention! You tend to achieve where you place your focus. This also extends to your family life as well. Dig deep and describe in your journal what your ideal home life looks like. Ask your family to get involved and contribute their visions as well. Not only will this open lines of communication it will also model for kids how to articulate what they really want in life and how to achieve their dreams. A win-win for everyone!

Use the following forms to help you identify areas in which you may want to enrich and enhance that will contribute to your overall life satisfaction and happiness.

Maintaining Balance

Balance is not about everything in your life receiving equal attention. It is about being mindful about where you need to place attention and energy at any given time. Your life is fluid and your attention should flow through the main areas of your life nurturing all aspects of life.

Label the following categories from 1 to 10, with 10 representing areas that are working well and 1 for areas that are not going so well in your life. (10=very satisfied, 1=not satisfied at all)

How satisfied are you with?

RELATIONSHIPS:

_____ Immediate Family (partner, children)

_____ Relationship with Yourself (body image, self-esteem, forgiveness, acceptance, trusting yourself, confidence level)

_____ Extended Family

_____ Friendships

_____ Spirituality

_____ Connection in the community.

_____ Your home.

WELLNESS:

_____ Health (physical, emotional, mental)

_____ Daily Movement (exercise, stretching, yoga, moving mindfulness, walking, etc.)

_____ Food Intake (Incorporating whole foods, water intake, relationship with food, etc.)

CAREER:

_____ I enjoy my job.

_____ My job allows me to fully express my passions and interests.

_____ I am in the right career field.

_____ I am satisfied with my salary, benefits package and time off.

LEISURE:

_____ I enjoy my leisure time.

_____ I use my leisure in productive, creative ways that enrich my life.

_____ I have fun in my spare time.

_____ I have enough spare time to do the things I enjoy most.

Results:

Seeing the areas of your life broken down in this way will give you an overview of the functioning level of each category. You can see which areas are working well and which areas may benefit from some attention. Anything over a seven is working well. As a general rule, anything under a five needs to be nurtured to increase satisfaction in that area. Ratings between five and seven can be addressed when the lower rated scores are brought up.

Use the next form to list your goals for increasing the lower rated categories.

Goal Setting

List goals and action steps you can take to increase satisfaction in identified categories from your Maintaining Balance assessment. Describe your goals using the SMART Goals approach as a guide.

S = Specific, describe your goals in detail

M = Measurable

A = Attainable

R = Relevant

T = Time oriented, place a timeframe that you will achieve your goals

Goal:

Describe in detail:

List 3 action steps you can take:

Describe how it will feel to reach your goal:

Goal:

Describe in detail:

List 3 action steps you can take:

Describe how it will feel to reach your goal:

Goal:

Describe in detail:

List 3 action steps you can take:

Describe how it will feel to reach your goal:

Place your goals where you will see them frequently. Focus on achieving small, incremental steps you can take to reach your goals. Consistent effort yields great results!

The program is over, now what?

Hopefully, you have learned positive ways to manage change and the often-accompanied worry and stress. There are many different facets to living. Now is the time to look at other aspects of your life in which you can enhance and grow. A life coach can help you get clear, stay focused and achieve your goals faster than if you were on your own. It feels good to have support and someone in which you can always bounce ideas. Your life coach is your biggest advocate, encouraging progress and supporting you through the bumps in the road on your way to reaching your most desired goals. For more information on life coaching please visit www.cindybakerlifedesign.com.

Epilogue

Each member showed up at the following monthly support group and shared what they had been up to since completing the class. Jerry was thrilled that his wife returned home two weeks ago. Even though Jerry returned to working outside of the home, he did follow through with his intention to delegate more work to his staff so he could cut back on his hours. Jerry said his wife, Mary, was happy that he was home more to do things as a family.

Even though Ann still misses her office life, she has adapted to working from home. She adjusted her work schedule to include more work travel to continue to build and maintain work relationships that are relevant for her position in the company.

Stephanie launched herself onto the personal growth path and has been reading self-help books. She told the group she is learning to accept herself more and as a result feels more peaceful and relaxed.

Rayna and Ginger have had a few coaching sessions together to help Rayna discover a career path that is in alignment with her passions, abilities, and interests. Oh, and Rayna finally got her dog to be quiet in her crate!

As for Miles, he still gets tense when people interrupt him; however, he says he uses the techniques and feels like he handles it better than he did in the past. Miles takes his work breaks as promised to spend time with his family.

Hopefully, you worked the steps along with Ann, Miles, Jerry, Rayna and Stephanie, and have used the information packets to support you in making helpful changes in your life as you work from home and manage family responsibilities. Practicing mindfulness is the foundation to managing stress that stems from big changes in your life. Working from home places new demands on your time and coming up with creative approaches and solutions to balance work and home is pivotal to cultivating peace, productivity, and joy. Filtering your reactions through the eyes of kindness, to yourself and others, will guide your responses to be more proactive and fruitful. Change is inevitable; however, using the tools taught in this book will decrease your stress as you become used to working and thriving from home.

About the Author

Cindy C. Baker is an established author in the field of self-development. She has a passion for helping others fulfill their own life path of peace, love, and genuine happiness. Cindy is a creative visionary with a powerful message to share with the world. Her passion has always been to make a positive impact, whether it be with an individual, group or business. She has a strong desire to help others feel valued, successful, and happy. Cindy has an artistic flair, often seeing opportunities where others may not. She has learned to listen to her deepest desires and consciously design her life and career on purpose. She possesses unique, eclectic qualities that demonstrate her exceptional ability to understand people that allow her to intuitively connect and build relationships, all with a sense of grounded practicality.

Cindy holds a master's degree (MA) in Psychology from Argosy University. She holds a Professional Counseling

License in Georgia and has been running her own private counseling practice for over ten years. In addition to being a counselor, she is a Board-Certified Coach (BCC) through the Center for Credentialing and Education. She has additional training in meditation and positive psychology. Cindy now guides clients through their own journey of self-discovery and teaches them how to design a life they love with a creative flair that makes her offerings one of a kind.

She can be reached at www.cindybakerlifedesign.com.

Access free resources that accompany the book at www.rockinlifefromhome.com.

www.ingramcontent.com/pod-product-compliance
Lightning Source LLC
Chambersburg PA
CBHW030913080526
44589CB00010B/278